BETHANY HAMILTON
Shark Attack Survivor

BY AMY VAN ZEE

Published by The Child's World®
1980 Lookout Drive • Mankato, MN 56003-1705
800-599-READ • www.childsworld.com

Acknowledgments
The Child's World®: Mary Berendes, Publishing Director
Red Line Editorial: Design, editorial direction, and production
Photographs ©: Matt Sayles/AP Images, cover, 1; iStockphoto, 4; D.Fujimoto/The
Garden Island/ZumaPress/Newscom, 7; Shutterstock Images, 8, 12, 21; Roberto
Westbrook/Blend Images/Corbis, 10; Splash News/Newscom, 14; Michael Darden/
West Hawaii Today/AP Images, 16, 18; Clifford White/Corbis, 20

ISBN 9781634074728

LCCN 2015946295

Printed in the United States of America
Mankato, MN
December, 2015
PA02286

ABOUT THE AUTHOR

Amy Van Zee is an editor and writer who lives with her family near
Minneapolis, Minnesota. She has an English degree from the University of
Minnesota and has contributed to dozens of educational books.

TABLE OF
CONTENTS

Chapter 1

A PASSION FOR SURFING

Huge waves crashed into the shore on the Hawaiian island of Oahu. It had been a good day for surfing at the Rell Sunn championships, an annual surfing contest on the island. And eight-year-old Bethany Hamilton was excited about it. That day, she had surfed the blue waves in her very first competition—and won. Two brand-new surfboards were her prizes. "Is this really happening to *me*?" she thought happily.[1]

Bethany was born to surf. Her parents, Tom and Cheri, met on the lush Hawaiian island of Kauai. They had each moved to Kauai from the U.S. mainland. They wanted to find better waves to surf. And they found them in Hawaii.

The Hamiltons passed on their love of surfing to their children. Bethany was born on February 8, 1990. She was surfing the Hawaiian waves by the time she was five. At that age, she still needed her parents' help in the water. But by age seven, she was surfing on her own. Her two older brothers, Noah and Timmy, enjoyed water sports, too. The whole family encouraged Bethany to be the best surfer she could be.

Bethany threw herself into the sport. She said, "Surfing is an addiction, a pleasure rush indescribable to anyone who has not experienced it. And when it grabs you, it won't let go." Bethany was hooked.[2]

Bethany did so well in her competitions that surf companies wanted to be her **sponsors**. Bethany was nine years old and an **amateur**. Having sponsors was a way for her to earn money.

5

This could help pay for her to surf. Traveling to each competition was expensive.

Bethany dreamed of being a professional surfer one day. She shared her passion with her friend Alana Blanchard. The two blond girls loved to surf the island's best spots together. They often faced each other in contests. But they cheered for one another. Bethany's parents taught her **sportsmanship**.

Bethany could spend a lot of time surfing because she was homeschooled. She could rise while it was still dark to surf as the sun came up. Then she would complete her schoolwork. It was a busy schedule. But Bethany's hard work brought results. In July 2003, Bethany placed second in a national surf championship. She was 13 years old.

LEARNING TO SURF

Children can start surfing as young as four years old, as long as they know how to swim. Many beginner surfers practice on the beach before they go out in the water. Beginners first learn how to jump up on the board, stand properly, and catch a wave. But the most important thing a child can learn when starting to surf is confidence in the water.

▲ **By the age of 10, Bethany already had four major companies sponsor her.**

Bethany woke early on the morning of October 31, 2003. It was 5:00 a.m. and the sun was not up yet. But as Bethany lay in bed, she hoped it would be a good day for surfing. Her mother, Cheri, suggested that they try a spot on the North Shore of

Kauai. As Bethany and her mother drove out in their old van, Bethany closed her eyes and enjoyed the smell of the flowers and the sea.

When they arrived, the waves were small, which is not good for surfing. But instead of going home, Bethany suggested that they walk to nearby Tunnels Beach. Just then, Bethany's friend Alana arrived. She had come to surf with her brother, Byron, and her father, Holt. Bethany's mother decided to head home. She told Bethany to get a ride home from Holt when they were done surfing. It wasn't the best day for surfing, but the ocean was blue and clear. The sand was warm. And Bethany was with her friends. She felt happy as she paddled out to sea. But what happened next changed her life forever.

◀ Tunnels Beach, also known as Makua Beach, is loved by tourists for snorkeling and by locals for surfing.

Chapter 2

SHARK ATTACK

Bethany, Alana, Byron, and Holt had been in the water for about 30 minutes. Bethany was farthest out in the water, lying on her surfboard. Her left arm floated in the ocean as she waited for a wave. Suddenly, Bethany sensed something big and gray creeping up on her left side. She felt pressure on her left arm as a huge tiger shark bit down and pulled her back and forth. It lasted only a few seconds. But the damage was serious.

The water around Bethany turned red. She knew her arm had been bitten off, but she didn't panic. Instead, she calmly called to her friends, "I just got attacked by a shark."[3] They saw the red water and Bethany's wound and quickly swam to her. Everyone tried to stay calm and focused on getting Bethany to the beach.

As they swam in, Holt took off his shirt and tied it around Bethany's wound as a **tourniquet**. He asked Bethany questions to keep her talking. It took 15 minutes to paddle to shore. Bethany prayed over and over. The shark could have returned to attack again, but it didn't.

Byron reached the shore first. He found a cell phone and dialed 911. When Holt, Alana, and Bethany got to the beach, a group gathered around. Bethany was lifted onto the sand. The people wrapped her in towels to keep her warm. Another surfer used his **surf leash** to make a tighter tourniquet for her arm.

Bethany was struggling to stay conscious. The pain in her arm was becoming intense. When Alana ran to get water for Bethany, she found a **paramedic** who was vacationing on the island with his family. He examined the wound and took Bethany's pulse.

▲ Tiger sharks are the second-most common sharks that attack humans, with great white sharks being the first.

He knew Bethany needed medical help, and fast. Finally, the ambulance arrived and Bethany was loaded in. It took her to Wilcox Memorial Hospital, a 45-minute drive away.

Bethany's father, Tom, was already at the hospital—but not for his daughter. Early that morning, he had gone to Wilcox for a simple knee surgery. Just as the doctors were about to begin, a nurse rushed in and said, "There's a 13-year-old girl coming, a shark attack victim. We are going to need this room right away."[4]

Tom's heart sank. He knew the victim had to be either Alana or his own daughter. The doctor told him it was Bethany. Tom's mind filled with worry as they wheeled him out. The doctors needed to get ready for her operation— her life was on the line.

FIGHTING BACK

The shark that attacked Bethany was about 14 feet (4 m) long. A shark's size, rows of teeth, and strong sense of smell make it a powerful predator. Sharks are drawn to blood in the water. Thrashing fish or a kicking swimmer could attract a shark's attention. But it is rare for a shark to attack a human. If it does happen, the person can fight back. Experts suggest trying to punch the shark in the face. Its eyes, nose, and gills are especially sensitive.

Chapter 3

A NEW LIFE

Waves of relief washed over Bethany. She had arrived at the hospital. Dr. David Rovinsky was waiting for her there. He would perform a surgery to help save Bethany's life. She had lost about half of her body's blood.

Bethany was put under with **anesthesia**. First, Dr. Rovinsky cleaned her wound to get rid of any germs left from the shark's mouth. Next, the doctor cut the nerves in her arm. Bethany still had a tiny bit of her arm left. But the wound was not yet closed up. The doctors wanted to make sure it did not become infected.

After her first surgery on Friday, friends and family filled her hospital room with balloons and flowers. On Sunday, a large group of friends from church came to visit. They prayed and sang with Bethany. She felt good and even thought about surfing again.

On Monday, Dr. Ken Pierce performed Bethany's second surgery. He closed the wound using extra skin from under Bethany's arm. The extra skin was held in place with stitches. The first time Bethany saw her wound and stitches after the surgery, she almost fainted. The reality of losing her arm began to sink in.

LOVE FOR BETHANY

Bethany's medical bills were expensive. On November 15, 2003, the island came together at a fundraiser for Bethany's family. The event had music, food, and items on which to bid. More than $75,000 was raised. Bethany also received encouraging mail from around the world, and some people sent money.

▲ After the shark attack, Bethany's dad made her a special surfboard that made it easier to paddle with one arm.

As part of her recovery, Bethany received **occupational therapy**. With only one arm, Bethany had to relearn many things, such as how to get dressed. But the doctor was hopeful. He felt that she would be able to do most of the things she had always done, but now with only her right arm.

While Bethany was recovering in the hospital, the news media heard about her story. Many newspapers and television stations wanted to hear more from her. The day after the attack, Bethany spoke about it to a local television station. By Tuesday, Bethany's story was on the front page of *The New York Times*. When she left the hospital on Wednesday, she had to leave through the back door to avoid the media. She stayed at a friend's house instead of her own. There were many reporters waiting at her house. She and her family needed peace and quiet.

After the attack, Bethany often shared that her faith in God is how she got through that difficult time. She had grown up going to a Christian church. She said in 2014, "I remember after I lost my arm, I just had this sense of peace that God was in control."[5] Bethany wanted to use her situation to tell people more about her beliefs. She thought maybe she could even help others through difficulties. And she would have lots of opportunities. But she had a goal for herself, too: to get back on the surfboard.

Chapter 4

BACK IN THE WATER

It was November 26, 2003. Bethany had been out of the ocean for almost a month. But she couldn't stay out any longer. She was determined to surf.

Bethany wrote that stepping back into the ocean was "like coming back home after a long, long trip."[6] Alana and her father were with Bethany in the water. And lots of friends had come to watch.

Bethany needed the encouragement. With only one arm, paddling and pushing herself up to stand was very difficult. She couldn't get the hang of it right away. But she kept trying. Finally, she stood up and rode her first wave. She was so happy that she cried.

Now that Bethany was back on the board, she focused on training. She got into a regular routine of exercise to become stronger. She practiced her technique, or specialized skill, with surf coaches. In 2005, Bethany won the National Scholastic Surfing Association Championships in the under-18 category. By 2008, Bethany was surfing professionally on the Women's Qualifying Series circuit. Her dream of becoming a professional surfer had come true.

By then, the story of Bethany's attack and her determination to surf again had made her famous. On November 21, 2003, she appeared on the news show *20/20*. On February 3, 2004, she told her story on *Oprah*. The show aired footage of her surfing with one arm. She traveled around the United States doing many more interviews. But all the attention was difficult at times. She was still just a teenager who liked to surf and spend time with friends.

19

▲ Bethany has traveled all over the world to surf in countries like Bali, Tahiti, and Australia, where she was surfing here in 2009.

And her friends urged Bethany to keep telling her story. Her book *Soul Surfer: A True Story of Faith, Family, and Fighting to Get Back on the Board* was released in 2004. In 2007, a documentary about her life was released. It was called *Heart of a Soul Surfer*. But something even bigger was in the works. The *Soul Surfer* book was made into a theatrical movie and released in 2011.

Bethany used her fame to help others. In 2005, she traveled to Thailand to help people who had suffered after a huge tsunami. Bethany helped the people feel safe in the water again. She taught surf lessons and played with the children. Bethany started a foundation called Friends of Bethany, which shares the message of Jesus with people who have lost limbs or who are facing other difficulties. And Bethany and Alana have also hosted an annual surf and games event for children on the island of Kauai.

Bethany continues to compete in surf competitions. In 2013, she was ranked in the top 50 female surfers in the world. That same year, Bethany married Adam Dirks, a youth minister. The couple welcomed a baby boy named Tobias in June 2015. As for surfing, Bethany once said in an interview, "I don't know how long I'll be competing but I'll always be surfing. I'll be surfing until I'm old."[7]

▲ Bethany with her husband, Adam Dirks, at the 2014 Nickelodeon Kids Choice Sports Awards.

GLOSSARY

amateur (AM-uh-chur): An amateur is a person who plays a sport for fun. When Bethany was an amateur surfer, she could not make money from her competitions.

anesthesia (a-nes-THEE-zhuh): Anesthesia is a person's loss of feeling in his or her body through the use of drugs. Bethany was under anesthesia for her surgery.

occupational therapy (ak-yuh-PAY-shun-ul THER-a-pee): Occupational therapy is a type of treatment that helps people learn to do everyday things. Bethany had occupational therapy to relearn how to do many things with one arm.

paramedic (pear-uh-MED-ic): A paramedic is a person who is trained to respond to a medical emergency. A paramedic helped Bethany while she waited for the ambulance to arrive.

sponsors (SPON-surs): Sponsors are companies that support an athlete with money or supplies. The money from Bethany's sponsors helped her family pay for traveling expenses.

sportsmanship (SPORTS-muhn-ship): Sportsmanship is when an athlete follows the rules of her sport, acts respectfully, and is a good loser. Bethany learned sportsmanship from her parents.

surf leash (SERF leesh): A surf leash is a device that connects a surfer's leg to the surfboard. A surfer tied his surf leash on Bethany's wounded arm to stop the bleeding.

tourniquet (TUR-ni-ket): A tourniquet is something that is tied around a wound to stop blood from flowing. A friend's dad made a tourniquet for Bethany's wound.

SOURCE NOTES

1. Bethany Hamilton. *Soul Surfer: A True Story of Faith, Family, and Fighting to Get Back on the Board*. New York: Gallery Books/MTV Books, 2001. Print. 42.

2. Ibid. 27.

3. Ibid. 71.

4. Ibid. 88.

5. Sasha Bogursky. "Surfer Bethany Hamilton on losing arm in shark attack: Jesus is my stronghold." *Fox News*. Fox News Network, LLC, 15 May 2014. Web. 12 Jun. 2015.

6. Hamilton. 180.

7. Emma John. "Riding the Storm." *The Guardian*. Guardian News Media Limited, 27 Jun. 2009. Web. 22 Jun. 2015.

TO LEARN MORE

Books

Green, Naima, and Hope Merlin. *An Insider's Guide to Surfing*. New York: Rosen Publishing, 2015.

Hamilton, Bethany, with Doris Rikkers. *Ask Bethany: FAQs: Surfing, Faith, and Friends*. Grand Rapids, MI: Zonderkidz, 2010.

Meloche, Renee Taft. *Bethany Hamilton: Riding the Waves*. Seattle, WA: YWAM Publishing, 2014.

Sandler, Michael. *Bethany Hamilton: Follow Your Dreams!* New York: Bearport Publishing, 2007.

Silbert, Jack. *Discovery Channel: The Big Book of Sharks*. New York: Time Home Entertainment, 2012.

Web Sites

Visit our Web site for links about Bethany Hamilton: childsworld.com/links

Note to Parents, Teachers, and Librarians: We routinely verify our Web links to make sure they are safe and active sites. So encourage your readers to check them out!

INDEX